Wind River

Stories™

YUSE
& the Spirit

A story by John Washakie

Illustrated by Jon Cox

Other **Wind River Stories**™ titles:

Coyote & the Rock
Crazy Man & the Plums
Fox & the Woodtick
Yuse, the Bully & the Bear

Published by Painted Pony, Inc. in association with the State of Wyoming
Copyright 2007 - Painted Pony, Inc.
All rights reserved
Printed by Global Interprint, Inc.
First Edition

ISBN - 0-9759800-3-7

Special thanks to:

Ft. Washakie Elementary School, students, faculty and administration
Jeston Edmo
Scott Ratliff
The Wyoming Department of Education
The Wind River Development Fund

Translations and captions by Cathy Shoyo Standing Rock & Manfred Guina, Sr.
Edited by Linda Stoval

P.O. Box 661
Ft. Washakie, WY 82514
www.paintedponyinc.com

Printed in Hong Kong

"This book is dedicated to Dewi and Nellie Washakie,
they never lost faith in me."

John Washakie

Forward

I grew up listening to stories told by my uncles, grandmothers, and parents. Many of the younger people today don't have someone to tell them stories and will never enjoy this learning experience. These stories have always been a way of passing on the cultural, history and religion of the Tribe and are the reason why I write.

This story is my gift to you.

John Washakie

It was spring and there was new life everywhere. The trees were green and the days were much longer. Yuse, once a chubby boy, was now a strong young brave of 14 winters. He felt the urge to travel.

He wanted to tell his parents about his plans to visit their Shoshone and Bannock relatives who lived on the other side of the Wind River Mountains. After their evening meal, Yuse decided it was a good time to talk about his plans.

Yuse ege chee daynah vican new

Yuse said, "Father, I am now a young man. I have some good horses and I want to travel to the west to visit some of our relatives."

Yuse glanced at his mother, expecting her to speak first. She did not say anything. His father was quiet, too, thinking about what he would say to Yuse.

F inally, Father said, "A trip over the mountains can be dangerous. There are wild animals like the bear, the mountain lion and rattlesnakes. Enemy warriors might attack you. There would be no one to help you."

Sond na-doe-comb-bay doe yah gudt

'They didn't say no, so there is still hope!' Yuse thought. He tried to think of something to say to convince them. He didn't have a good answer, so he decided to wait. Father had a habit of talking out loud when he made decisions about his children. He said that he did this so everyone would know all of the facts he had considered.

N ow, there was silence in the teepee. Father seemed to be at a loss for words. Yuse felt sure that Father knew he could take care of himself. To Mother's disappointment, Father said, "Yuse, you are strong and brave. Take a couple of good horses and enough supplies for a week." Yuse beamed with appreciation and pride.

Yuse uh upah yekwi, un-uh me uh

Y use was up early the next morning and went down by the river where the horses were held at night. He caught two horses that he could either ride or pack. When he got back to camp, Mother was waiting with his supplies packed in a rawhide case. She had done this many times for Father.

Like Father, Yuse rode up to Mother and jumped off his horse. He picked up the case and lashed it on his packhorse. He was ready and very excited, but had one last thing to do. He went to Mother and gave her a big hug.

Yuse ma be ah kwa vake

Yuse swung onto his horse, grabbed the lead rope of the packhorse and headed for the north trail across the Warm Valley. It would be a long ride this first day. He wanted to get as far away from camp as possible, just in case Father changed his mind and sent someone to bring him home.

he north trail was the shortest route to Towgotee Pass. The ride across Warm Valley was hot and dusty. Several times when the trail came near the Big Wind River, Yuse stopped and watered the horses.

Dee he yah, bah su wandt, uh-deen-t da vah

By late afternoon, Yuse left the foothills and started climbing through the tall pine trees. He thought about making camp, but for some reason he kept going. Just before dark he reached the top of the mountain and made camp there.

The trail down the other side was too dangerous to use at night. He would be risking injury to himself or his horses if he tried it.

Y use unpacked the horses and tied them to a tree. He quickly gathered wood to make a campfire. "High on this mountain it will be cold tonight. A hot meal before sleeping will help," Yuse said to himself.

Yuse doiyagine huupi muh waiharde

It was completely dark now and the moon would not rise until later. Yuse prepared his meal by the flickering light of the campfire. He made some herb tea in one pot and a stew of deer meat and wild potatoes in the other. The stew would take some time, so he leaned back on a big boulder to rest.

Yuse havi muh waiharde gudt

Yuse thought about Towgotee Pass and the Sheepeater Tribe that had taught other Tribes about it. The Sheepeaters were very friendly and peace-loving people who lived in the high mountains.

Dim bee divo puh, soo dee dukoo duka, divo ie dapp

There the water flowed either to the east and became the Big Wind River or to the west and became the Snake River. It was amazing to think about this. Each drop of water went either east or west from the top of the mountains. Together they created mighty rivers.

Y use caught the smell of his stew and knew it was almost ready to eat. He was about to put another stick on the fire when he heard a sound in the dark. He sat very still listening to the sound.

Yuse, hee-need-ah nugundt do-ya dug

'What is that?' he thought. He listened even harder. It sounded like a horse walking. 'Probably a rider saw my campfire. I would enjoy some company,' he thought.

Then the sound stopped. Yuse stared into the darkness, but saw nothing. At last, with the light from the moon, he saw the silhouette of a person on horseback.

Yuse uvaise edunt ah dah-vich en dick gah

The custom of the Shoshone is to welcome strangers. Yuse was frightened, but managed to say, "Please put up your horse and join me for a meal."

The stranger did not speak, but turned his horse and disappeared into the dark. It was odd because the horse and rider made no sound when they left. Yuse didn't know what to do. He waited, not moving or making a sound. He had been taught to never be afraid of anyone or anything that comes in a friendly way. Yuse worked hard to not be afraid.

A few minutes later, a stranger appeared out of the dark and stood by the fire. The stranger was completely wrapped in a beautiful blanket from head to foot.

Ideeq ahdahvich zandt navunde eh gundt

S urprised, but remembering his manners, Yuse said, "Sit down and I will give you a bowl of stew and a cup of tea." He could not see any part of the stranger - just his blanket.

The stranger sat down on the rock with his back to the fire and said nothing. Yuse poured a cup of tea and offered it to the stranger. "Here is some tea for you," he said.

The stranger shifted his body a little bit, then there was movement in one of the blanket folds. Yuse almost dropped the cup when he saw the hand! It was a skeleton's hand! Yuse's heart was pounding.

*Ideeq **ah dahvich ah** na doe comb bay*

'This is no human. This is one of the wandering spirits I have heard about,' he thought. Yuse took a deep breath and put the cup of tea in the skeleton hand without spilling a drop.

T he spirit again turned its back and Yuse could hear it drinking the tea. He filled a bowl with stew and said, "Here is your stew."

Again the figure shifted and the hand appeared out of the fold. Yuse quickly delivered the stew. Now, the spirit turned to the fire and began eating.

Y use was so frightened that he almost spilled his stew. He was afraid, but there was nothing he could do. He began to eat his food - and it was good.

When he had finished the stew, he thought again of the Shoshone custom. "You are welcome to spend the night. You can sleep on that side of the fire and I will make my bed on this side of the fire," he offered.

Yuse mah na doe comb bay sa-pundt hagu muh u-puih-duh

Slowly, the spirit turned toward Yuse. Bony hands appeared out of the blanket. They moved slowly up and pulled the blanket down exposing its skull. Yuse swallowed hard. He had never been this scared, but he did not move or speak.

Yuse mu dent na doe comb bay deyant

F inally, the spirit spoke, "Friend, where are you going?"

Yuse answered, speaking very fast, "I am going to visit my relatives, the Shoshone and Bannock people. They live far to the west of here."

The Spirit nodded and began making a bed of his blanket. 'So, the spirit is staying the night,' Yuse thought. Then he quickly made his bed and crawled in. He lay in silence watching the stars until well after the fire had burned out.

When Yuse fell asleep, he had a dream. It was an amazing dream. He was riding his horse and leading his packhorse. He was following the spirit, but the horses were not walking or running. The horses were flying high over the pine trees!

Yuse zandt na vee showup

T he moon was setting and he could see the Tetons far in the distance.

He was so awed by the beauty of the view that he could only stare down in wonder. The Tetons faded from view behind them. He looked toward the east and the sun was just appearing on the distant skyline. Yuse looked back to the west and the spirit and its horse were gone. He was so startled that he awoke from his dream.

Yuse davasivaitsuk devuih davadoine benike

To his surprise, he was not in his bed by the campfire. He was on horseback leading his packhorse down a hill. And there, by the bank of the Snake River, was the village of his relatives. He kept blinking his eyes and slapping his leg trying to wake himself up.

Yuse mitetsih mah nanrewenr katayne

Then he realized that the dream had been real. It was as the older people said, "Befriend a good spirit and you will be rewarded. Scare it away and harm will come to you or your family."

Y use was still thinking about his experience with the Spirit when someone called his name. He looked and saw some of his cousins running toward him.

"Hello!" Yuse called.

"How was your journey?" his cousin asked.

"It was…amazing!" Yuse answered.

It was a truly amazing experience that Yuse would never forget.

Glossary

Shoshone Word	English Word
1. na-dent	danger
2. qa vuck	hug
3. dee he yah	horses
4. hoop	wood
5. doe yeah	mountain
6. way-hande	fire
7. doeyah dug	forest
8. dee und	frightened
9. uh dah vich	stranger
10. eh	blanket
11. na doe comb bay	spirit
12. nai we shund	dream

Illustration Captions in Shoshone Language

Page 9. Yuse ege chee daynah vican new
　　　　Yuse is older now

Page 11. Sond na-doe-comb-bay doe yah gudt
　　　　There are many dangers in the mountains

Page 13. Yuse uh upah yekwi, un-uh me uh
　　　　Father decides Yuse may go

Page 15. Yuse ma be ah kwa vake
　　　　Yuse hugs his mother

Page 17. Dee he yah, bah su wandt, uh-deen-t da vah
　　　　The horses need water when it is hot

Page 19. Yuse doiyagine huupi muh waiharde
　　　　Yuse gathers wood for fire

Page 20. Yuse havi muh waiharde gudt
　　　　Yuse rests by the campfire

Page 21. Dim bee divo puh, soo dee dukoo duka, divo ie dapp
　　　　Rock art of the Sheep Eaters

Page 23. Yuse, hee-need-ah nugundt do-ya dug
　　　　Yuse hears something in the forest

Page 24. Yuse uvaise edunt ah dah-vich en dick gah
　　　　Yuse invites the stranger to eat

Page 26. Ideeq ahdahvich zandt navunde eh gundt
　　　　The stranger has a beautiful blanket

Page 28. Ideeq ah dahvich ah na doe comb bay
　　　　The stranger is really a spirit

Page 32. Yuse mah na doe comb bay sa-pundt hagu muh u-puih-duh
　　　　Yuse shows the spirit where to sleep

Page 33. Yuse mu dent na doe comb bay deyant
　　　　Yuse is frightened by the spirit

Page 36. Yuse zandt na vee showup
　　　　Yuse has an amazing dream

Page 38. Yuse davasivaitsuk devuih davadoine benike
　　　　Yuse woke up and saw the sun

Page 39. Yuse mitetsih mah nanrewenr katayne
　　　　Yuse was near his cousin's village

John R. Washakie

Before John started writing, he spent 18 years on the Eastern Shoshone Business Council. While on the Council, he made numerous presentations to the House of Representatives and Senate Select Committee on Indian Affairs. He was appointed by 3 different Department of Interior Secretaries to serve on several national committees to address issues from Reorganization of the Bureau of Indian Affairs to Energy policy. He is the great grandson of Chief Washakie whose statue resides in the rotunda of the U.S. Capitol. He earned a B.A. in History from the University of Wyoming. He is a veteran of the Vietnam War.

He claims to be an average writer and just a good listener when his grandmother, uncles, or anyone else told stories. With the tradition of storytelling being almost gone, John decided he must use the new technologies of computers, printing and publishing to save these stories so that they would once again be passed on.

John was born and raised in Fort Washakie, Wyoming where he currently lives with his wife, Bonnie. They have three children, Tonya, Joe and Candace. They also have thirteen grandchildren, Kyle, Kristen, Kayle, Chase, Cathy, Wekota, Hailey, Jackie, Yvonne, Kailyn, Kanani, Kenny, Keeley.

Jon T. Cox

I grew up in Cheyenne, Wyoming and graduated from East High School, The University of Wyoming and most importantly, the school of life. I have had a variety of occupations and been many things in my time. I owe a great deal of these experiences, successes and strengths to my parents, sister, brother and family. My wife Tammy and my children, Kelly, Katy and Jon have allowed me to be whatever I dreamed. I love them all. From the experience of raising and contributing to a family, one learns a lot about life and the lessons it presents for passage through it. Another passion and love of mine is gardening. My wife has taught me a great deal about it and is the real gardener. I am really just the lawn boy.

One of the people who taught me other important lessons in life was Professor Victor Flach, who directed my Masters' program. He believed that we must make a record of our experiences. If we do not, then we must ask, did they ever happen? Although only a story, this book is a record and vital part of Native American culture that must not be allowed to disappear. I consider it a privilege to have been allowed to record this traditional story through my illustrations.

As for John Washakie, he is not one to talk about himself or his accomplishments. He is above all a great listener and because of that, he has learned many wonderful stories that colorfully teach life's lessons. This is one of them and if you listen well enough, you too will learn a great deal.

Jon Cox